SIR MICHAEL PARKINSON

AN UNBELIEVABLE JOURNEY OF MEETINGS AND MOTIVATION

KING SMARTY

SIR MICHAEL PARKINSON

SIR MICHAEL PARKINSON

Table Of Content

Introduction

Sir Michael Parkinson, an English television personality well known for meeting stars including Muhammed Ali, John Wayne, Tom Journey, Madonna, and Sir Paul McCartney on his syndicated program Parkinson, has passed on. He was 88.

Parkinson's family gave an assertion to the BBC on Thursday morning that he had passed on "calmly" following a "brief sickness."
"After a short illness, Sir Michael Parkinson died calmly at home last evening in the company of his family," the assertion said.
"The family demands that they are given security and time to lament."
A delegate for Parkinson didn't quickly answer Individuals' solicitations for input.

Parkinson was brought into the world in Yorkshire, Britain, in 1935, per the BBC, and served in the English armed forces prior to turning into a columnist.

His show, Parkinson, was previously broadcast on the BBC in 1971 and ran for quite a long time. In 1998, the show got back to the BBC until 2003, before moving over to equal channel ITV until 2007.

During his time facilitating his visit show, Parkinson talked with many stars, remembering entertainer Wayne for 1974.

In one critical trade, the host examined Wayne concerning the purported Hollywood Boycott—a rundown of the people who supposedly had associations with the Socialist Coalition—provoking the entertainer to reject that anybody was boycotted.

Other eminent interviewees included fighter Ali, who showed up on Parkinson at numerous events; Tom Hanks; David Bowie;

Victoria and David Beckham; Will Smith; Gwyneth Paltrow; and George Clooney.

In recognition of Parkinson, who was knighted by Sovereign Elizabeth in 2008, BBC Chief General Tim Davie depicted the host as "the lord of the talk show" and said that Parkinson "characterized the organization for every one of the moderators and shows that followed."

"He talked with the greatest stars of the twentieth century and did as such, which enchanted the general population. Michael was not just splendid at seeking clarification on pressing issues; he was likewise a brilliant audience," Davie added

He proceeded, "Michael was genuinely exceptional, a mind-blowing telecaster and writer who will be colossally missed."

English humorist Eddie Izzard likewise honored the television show on X, previously known as Twitter, on Thursday morning.

"It is extremely miserable to hear that Michael Parkinson has left us. He was the lord of the insightful meeting," Izzard, 61, composed

Parkinson got therapy for prostate malignant growth in 2013, and specialists gave him the all-reasonable treatment in 2015, as per the BBC.

He is made due by his better half, Mary Parkinson, whom he wed in 1959, and his three kids: Andrew, Nicholas and Michael Jr.

Chapter 1

The Yorkshire Beginnings

In the quiet scene of Yorkshire, Britain, on a fresh harvest day, September 28, 1935, the world invited a spirit bound to exceed all expectations some day. Michael Parkinson's entry into the world denoted the start of a day-to-day existence that would make a permanent imprint on the domain of media and diversion.

Experiencing childhood in the embrace of a humble family, youthful Michael's initial years were shaded by the charming stories told by his folks and the encompassing open country. It was in this supportive climate that his regular interest and love for narrating flourished. Indeed, even as a kid, his propensity for retelling stories and describing ordinary occasions stamped him as a sprouting scholar and communicator.

The rambling scenes and curious towns of Yorkshire, with their natural appeal and quiet excellence, gave him material on which his creative mind thrived. Every little hiding spot held an expected story, and each experience with a bystander offered a chance for association. It was in these early stages that Michael's partiality for noticing human instinct and his natural capacity to produce associations were sharpened.

As the seasons spun and the years progressed, the kid who once paid attention to the stories of others started making his own accounts. His school years were set apart by an enthusiasm to partake in discussions, show clubs, and any open door that permitted him to verbally communicate his thoughts. His enthusiasm for correspondence was clear in each word he expressed, each line he conveyed, and each story he shared.

The humble environmental factors of Yorkshire might have been a long way from the terrific stages and splendid lights that would later turn into his scenery, but they provided the establishment whereupon his renowned lifetime was fabricated. As time passed, he drew motivation from the scenes and individuals that encompassed him, supporting his hunger for information and his devotion to the craft of discussion.

In the core of Yorkshire, in the midst of the moving slopes and curious towns, Michael Parkinson's process started. The seeds of interest, narrating, and association that were planted in those early years would ultimately bloom into a vocation that would reclassify the specialty of talking and make a permanent imprint on the universe of diversion. As the breezes of predetermination murmured through the Yorkshire valleys, they conveyed with them the commitment of significance, making way for a noteworthy life that would unfold with each passing section.

Chapter 2

From Officer to Scribe

As the unavoidable trends moved throughout the years, young Michael's process veered off in a strange direction. In a show of obligation and nationalism, he addressed the call to serve his nation, assuming the uniform of the English armed forces. The military, with its organized schedules and interest in discipline, would give him important life illustrations that would shape his direction in ways he would never have envisioned.

Wrapped up in the fellowship and difficulties of military life, Michael leveled up his inborn initiative abilities. The discipline he gained during this period would become an indispensable piece of his personality, impacting his way of dealing with future undertakings. The steady quest for greatness and the resolute obligation to his obligations laid the foundation for his future victories.

Upon the completion of his tactical help, Michael ended up at a junction. The very enthusiasm that had pushed him through the positions of the military presently encouraged another energy inside him—an affection for the composed word. Embracing his intrinsic interest and desire to impart, he progressed from the universe of outfits and orders to the domain of newscasting.

With a pen close by and a heart brimming with stories, Michael set out on an excursion into the universe of detail. His sharp observational abilities, sharpened during his tactical days, demonstrated significant value as he dove into his new job. Similarly, as he had paid attention to the stories of his folks and neighbors in his childhood, he now pays attention to the heartbeat of his general surroundings, searching out stories that resonate with the human experience.

Through his words, he laid out striking pictures of people and occasions, permitting perusers to travel close by him as he uncovered secret bits of insight and untold accounts. The very assurance and commitment that had driven him in the military now fill his quest for editorial greatness. With each article he wrote, he educated as well as associated with his perusers, exhibiting his capacity to connect holes through the force of the composed word.

As the ink moved from his pen, Michael's standing as a gifted scribe developed. His capacity to make convincing stories drew consideration, and his articles turned into a wellspring of motivation and thought for some. Through his composition, he showed a novel gift for catching the substance of a second and meshing it into an embroidery of human inclination.

The change from fighter to recorder denoted an extraordinary stage in Michael's life. The discipline and initiative developed during his tactical help mixed consistently with his regular interest and compassion, creating a powerful range of abilities that would prepare him for his future undertakings. Much to his dismay, this excursion into the domain of newscasting was just the start—an introduction to the remarkable way that would lead him to reclassify the scene of TV facilitation and discussion.

Chapter 3

The Introduction of "Parkinson"

It was 1971, and the English TV scene was on the cusp of an extraordinary shift. Little did the world have at least some idea that another first light was going to break—a sunrise that would be set apart by the presence of an exclusive who might reshape the specialty of discussion on TV until the end of time.

Right then and there, "Parkinson" made its introduction—a syndicated program that would rise above diversion and become a stage for significant exchange. Michael Parkinson ventured onto the screen not just as a host but rather as a guide for discussions that would reverberate through the chronicles of history.

With a gleam in his expression and a glow in his voice, Michael invited viewers into a reality where VIP interviews were not generally restricted to shallow trades. All things considered, they became private discussions that stripped back the layers of popularity, uncovering the humanity underneath. His special capacity to associate with individuals, a gift sharpened during his time in the military and his excursion as a writer, was currently displayed for a fantastic scope.

As the show unfolded, the crowd demonstrated the veracity of Michael's dominance in the specialty of interviews. Outfitted with examining questions that dove past the surface, he uncovered stories that hadn't been shared previously—a demonstration of his real interest and commitment to grasping the human experience. His methodology wasn't that of a questionnaire, but of an inquisitive pilgrim, anxious to uncover the secret fortunes inside every visitor's excursion.

From Hollywood stars to prestigious performers, from powerful legislators to social symbols, "Parkinson" was a blend of different voices, points of view, and stories. Michael's sympathetic listening created an air of trust, empowering his visitors to open up and share their considerations, dreams, and weaknesses. In his presence, famous people shed their public personas and became engaging people, making every episode a revelation for watchers around the world.

His meetings weren't only snapshots of diversion; they were windows into the spirits of the individuals who graced his stage. Whether it was an impactful trade about existence's preliminaries and wins or a loud chuckling prompting story, Michael explored the range of feelings with artfulness, genuineness, and beauty. The real associations produced during those meetings rose above the screen, leaving a permanent effect on both visitors and viewers.

Michael Parkinson's "Parkinson " turned out to be in excess of a network show—it was a social peculiarity. It re-imagined the specialty of talking, hoisting it to a new and groundbreaking level. With every episode, he demonstrated that an expert questioner was not simply an examiner but rather a narrator who could catch the substance of an individual's life in practically no time.

As the show's particular tune played and the credits rolled, the effect of "Parkinson" reverberated a long way past the limits of the screen. With his real interest, compassionate tuning in, and capacity to cultivate certified associations, Michael had turned into the encapsulation of an expert questionnaire, everlastingly drawing his name throughout the entire existence of TV and discussion.

Chapter 4

Symbols in Conversation

Inside the walls of the "Parkinson" studio, Michael Parkinson invited a procession of illuminators that had made history. The stage turned into a sacrosanct space where legends strolled and where, under Michael's masterful direction, interviews rose above into immortal discourses that would perpetually stay carved in the embroidery of diversionary history.

Perhaps the most famous discussion that graced the "Parkinson" stage was with, as a matter of fact, Muhammad Ali. The charming fighter's awesome presence was met with Michael's authentic appreciation and regard. As they exchanged words and shared stories, the meeting changed into a dance of mind and shrewdness. Through their trade, watchers got a brief look at the man behind the legend, the contender who stood in the boxing ring as well as against social treachery and imbalance.

The cryptic David Bowie likewise graced the stage, uncovering his complex persona through genuine disclosures. Michael's keen inquiries dove into the profundities of Bowie's inventive flow, permitting viewers to look into the psyche of a melodic virtuoso. The discussion uncovered layers of imaginativeness and weakness, exhibiting the many-sided woven artwork of feelings that filled Bowie's innovative excursion.

In the domain of film, Tom Hanks carried his appeal and lowliness to the "Parkinson" stage. Their discussion went beyond examining films; it dove into the quintessence of narrating and the entertainer's association with his jobs. Michael's capacity to establish a climate of trust and affinity permitted Hanks to get serious about his specialty, uncovering the commitment and enthusiasm that energized his exhibitions.

The universe of sports was additionally investigated through Michael's meetings with incredible figures like George Best and Sir Bobby Charlton. The meetings weren't just about triumphs and losses; they laid out a picture of people whose lives were woven with wins and difficulties, both on and off the field.

The social scene was improved by his discussions with craftsmen like Sir Paul McCartney, whose tales and bits of knowledge into the universe of music uncovered the enchantment behind the tunes. The screen turned into a material, whereupon the magnificence of McCartney's manifestations and the energy driving his creativity were painted for all to observe.

Through these discussions, Michael's interesting range of abilities as a questioner sparkled. His capacity to pose intriguing inquiries while maintaining an air of solace and realness permitted his visitors to strip back the layers, uncovering their humanity. The "Parkinson" stage wasn't simply a stage for stars; it was a mirror reflecting the common encounters and feelings that interface with every one of us.

With every visitor, Michael excelled at catching their embodiment, be it their accomplishments, battles, or yearnings. The "Parkinson" interviews were more than simple features of VIP; they were certified trades that changed the unremarkable into the exceptional, uncovering that the existence of symbols was interlaced with the human experience. Under Michael's masterful direction, these discourses enlightened the hearts and psyches of the stars, and in doing so, they enlightened the spirits of the watchers too.

Chapter 5

Characterizing Moments

In the rich embroidery of "Parkinson," woven with endless discussions that reverberated with crowds, one specific discourse sparkled like a diamond: Michael's trade with the unbelievable John Wayne. This interview would proceed to characterize the show as well as Michael's brave way to deal with exploring the mind-boggling interchange between amusement and cultural issues.

As John Wayne, the notable figure known for his transcending presence and rough appeal, subsided into his seat opposite Michael, an atmosphere of expectation wrapped the studio. The air was accused of being the quintessence of a true-to-life period that had made a permanent imprint on history.

The discussion started with the normal discussion about Wayne's renowned filmography—an excursion through the scenes of Hollywood's brilliant years. However, it was Michael's relentless obligation to the art of meeting that elevated this experience beyond the conventional. With a ready yet conscious disposition, he wandered into an unfamiliar area, examining the supposed Hollywood Boycott, a subject that had been covered in discussion and mystery.

As the inquiry lingered palpably, the world paused its breathing. It was a request that requested mental fortitude—an inquiry that addressed the political unrest of the time as well as the complex harmony between the opportunity of articulation and the obligation of individuals of note.

Wayne, a symbol of tough independence, figured out the inquiry. His reaction was his very own demonstration of convictions, as well as a brief look into the intricacies of a period set apart by doubt and vulnerability. What might have been a strained conflict changed into a nuanced trade, uncovering layers of individual and cultural history.

This vital crossroads exhibited Michael's striking skill to overcome any issues between big names and reality. His brave exploration of sensitive themes addressed his commitment to truth and validity. He didn't avoid the awkwardness; all things being equal, he turned it into a chance for certified discourse. In doing so, he displayed his expertise as an expert director, coordinating discussions that reverberated with both the people at the center of attention and the endless watchers at home.

This meeting with John Wayne wasn't one minute of TV; it was a demonstration of the force of correspondence. Michael's methodology filled in as an update that, underneath the exciting facade of popularity and fame, there were human encounters, feelings, and viewpoints that merited investigation. It was an illustration of the specialty of posing inquiries not exclusively to illuminate but also to encourage understanding—a quality that put Michael aside as a genuine illuminator in the domain of questionnaires.

As the cameras rolled and the exchange proceeded, the world looked as Michael explored the scarce difference between veneration and request. This discussion made a permanent imprint on the hearts and brains of the people who gave testimony, a demonstration of the boldness, validity, and compassion that characterized Michael's way to deal with his specialty.

Chapter 6

A Knighted Legacy

In the records of acknowledgment and honor, a zenith second anticipated Sir Michael Parkinson—one that wouldn't just recognize his unmatched commitments to broadcasting and reporting but in addition set his status as a treasured mainstay of English culture. It was in the year 2008 that Sovereign Elizabeth II presented to him the title of knighthood, a qualification that raised him to a domain of highly regarded people who had made a permanent imprint on the structure holding the system together.

The fresh insight about Sir Michael's knighthood resounded like a resonating note, resounding through the hearts of admirers who had followed his excursion from the starting points of "Parkinson" to the profundities of its most significant discussions. With the distinction of knighthood came the impression of a vocation set apart by devotion, development, and a pledge to cultivate real associations.

As the instruction service unfolded, Sir Michael remained on the edge of history, clad in the formal attire that represented his new position. The knight's honor was a demonstration of his capacity to overcome any issues between universes, whether it was the universe of the conventional individual or that of the phenomenal light. With his particular appeal and modesty, he acknowledged the honor not just as his very own acknowledgment of accomplishments but additionally as a sign of approval for the specialty of discussion itself.

The knighthood commended his own process as well as the groundbreaking force of media and correspondence. Through his meetings, Sir Michael had permitted people in general to see the lives, dreams, and goals of symbols. In doing so, he had turned into a nonentity of a social shift—one that focused on validity, sympathy, and exchange in a time frequently characterized by triviality.

Sir Michael's knighthood wasn't simply an honor given to him; it was an honor that reached out to every one of the individuals who had been moved by his work. It was a sign of approval for the aggregate enthusiasm for his creativity, his devotion to truth, and his obligation to investigate the complex elements of the human experience. His inheritance was presently interwoven with the tradition of English culture itself—a heritage that would keep on moving people in the future of columnists, telecasters, and questionnaires.

As the drapery closed on the induction service, Sir Michael Parkinson ventured forward as a knight, a minister of discussion, and a gatekeeper of credibility. His process had taken him from the unassuming scenes of Yorkshire to the fabulous phases of TV and, presently, to the distinguished positions of knighthood. In presenting this title, Sovereign Elizabeth II had not just perceived a man; she had praised a heritage — a perseverance through demonstration of the extraordinary force of words, association, and the craft of tuning in.

Chapter 7

Past the Show

As the last drapery fell on "Parkinson," denoting the conclusion of an important time period, the effect of Sir Michael's impact kept on resonating a long way past the limits of the studio. The inheritance he had carefully woven through many years of discussions, giggling, and contemplation broadened its ring, molding the actual pitch of interview strategies and TV shows for a long time into the future.

The reverberations of his curious nature, warm disposition, and capacity to produce associations waited in the air, filling in as a directing light for arising moderators and questionnaires. As the years progressed, Michael created a plan for an alternate sort of discussion—one that went past the practiced responses and lustrous façades.

He had shown that realness was the foundation of significant communications, and his heritage lighted a change in outlook in the realm of media.

Another generation of hosts emerged, motivated by his methodology. They embraced his ethos, looking for short clips, yet stories; titles, yet genuine trades. His capacity to cause visitors to feel seen and heard turned into the highest quality level in the business, encouraging a climate where weakness and real association flourished.

The effect of his heritage was clear in the actual texture of the TV show. The times of simply dramatic meetings were winding down, traded by a longing for substance and profundity. Michael's impact had ignited a change that provoked questionnaires to dig further, pose awkward inquiries, and explore the complicated landscape of human encounters.

The once-extremist thought of cultivating significant exchange in a media scene frequently overwhelmed by emotionalism and triviality turned into the new standard. Michael's heritage had delivered validity with its very own money, and crowds requested nothing less. The change was obvious; discussions became stages for knowledge, compassion, and verifiable investigation.

In any case, Michael's heritage wasn't restricted to the domain of television shows and meetings. His methodology, described with interest and regard, saturated different aspects of media, enhancing narratives, digital broadcasts, and, surprisingly, editorial examinations. The idea of "talking with" extended to embrace narrating in its most perfect structure—a workmanship that permitted people to uncover their excursions, weaknesses, and wins.

The gradually expanding influences of Michael's heritage came across lines and societies. His capacity to connect holes through discussion rose above language hindrances, demonstrating that real human association is an all-inclusive yearning. His lessons turned into a standard for writers, telecasters, and narrators around the world, helping them to remember the extraordinary force of a very well-created question and a listening ear.

As the years passed, Michael's heritage kept on sparkling brilliantly, a directing star for the people who looked to convey and interface. Through the developments he spearheaded, the discussions he worked with, and the associations he supported, Sir Michael Parkinson had made a permanent imprint on the craft of correspondence—an inheritance that would everlastingly shape the scene of meetings and TV shows, a persevering through update that each discussion, regardless of how little, has the ability to influence hearts, minds, and the actual world.

Chapter 8

The Last Curtain

As the ways of the world kept on moving, Sir Michael Parkinson's process was set apart by the two victories and preliminaries, filling in as a demonstration of his unflinching soul and the flexibility that had come to characterize his wonderful vocation.

As time passed, he remained a resolute presence in the hearts of admirers and a guiding light for the people who looked for verifiable associations thanks to discussion. His heritage had solidified him as a paragon of bona fide correspondence, an illustration of how to explore the intricacies of human connection with elegance and compassion.

However, as life so frequently unfolded, challenges arose along the way. Among them was an impressive for—prostate malignant growth. Notwithstanding this fight, Sir Michael exhibited the very characteristics that had made him a symbol: a mix of assurance, mental fortitude, and the capacity to explore life's pinnacles and valleys with enduring flexibility.

Like the interviewees who had shared their accounts on his stage, Sir Michael set out on his very own excursion—one that required weakness, strength, and an eagerness to face the unexplored world. His conclusion was met not with router but rather with a steely purpose to face the sickness head-on, similarly to how he had explored extreme inquiries and sensitive subjects all through his profession.

The very curious nature that had filled his discussions turned into the main impetus as he looked for the most ideal treatment and battled to recover his well being. Fully backed up by his friends and family, the clinical local area, and the unfaltering consolation of his admirers, he set out on an excursion set apart by trust and assurance.

Through medicines and difficulties, Sir Michael never failed to focus on his motivation—a reason that had risen above the screen and become a guide for association. His fight with malignant growth turned into a part of his biography that spoke not exclusively to his own versatility but also to the strength that rises out of the obligations of the local area and shared encounters.

Also, similarly to what he had done all through his vocation, Sir Michael arose triumphant. With the very assurance that had described his discussions, he dealt with misfortune directly and arose on the opposite side—his soul whole, his inheritance flawless. His excursion through sickness and recuperation turned into a demonstration of the actual pith of his being—an update that life is a progression of discussions, some spoken resoundingly and others conveyed in the heart, all adding to the mind-boggling embroidery of the human experience.

As the last shade moved closer, the world kept on being moved by the unyielding soul of Sir Michael Parkinson. His story filled in as a guide to motivation for that large number of people confronting their own difficulties, a demonstration of the force of versatility, genuineness, and the rugged string of human association.

Chapter 9

An Enduring Impression

As the sun set on a calm night, a section of Sir Michael Parkinson's existence was attracted to a nearby At 88 years old, encompassed by the affection and warmth of his dearest family, he set out on an excursion that rose above reality. In his last minutes, his soul found comfort in the hug of the people who had shared his excursion, both on screen and in the domain of life itself.

Insight about his passing spread like waves in a lake, conveying with it a feeling of misfortune that touched the hearts of individuals across the globe. The heritage he had woven, each discussion in turn, was not lost in his flight. All things being equal, it bloomed into getting through embroidery—a demonstration of the force of association, understanding, and compassion.

Accolades poured in from each edge of the world—from associates who had shared his stage, admirers who had been moved by his words, and individual performers who had seen his dominance. Every recognition was a brushstroke on the material of a daily existence that had made a permanent imprint, a day-to-day existence that had raised the demonstration of discussion to a fine art.

The world celebrated the host, yet the inheritance he had abandoned Through his meetings, he had deified the accounts, battles, and victories of innumerable people. He had caught the passing embodiment of minutes that could have, in any case, been lost to time. His capacity to distill the human experience into strong trades had touched hearts and mixed spirits in ways unimaginable.

In a time portrayed by short-lived patterns and transient minutes, Sir Michael Parkinson's effect was persevering—an update that real discussions hold the ability to rise above ages. The discussions he had worked with were more than interviews; they were a demonstration of the magnificence of shared stories, the strength of weakness, and the extraordinary idea of human association.

As the world bid goodbye to Sir Michael Parkinson, his legacy was scratched in the chronicles of TV history as well as in the hearts of all who had been moved by his presence. He had re-imagined the specialty of discussion, changed interviews into exchanges, and made a permanent imprint on the scene of media and correspondence.

The last section of his story wasn't an end, but a continuation of the significant effect he had on the world. The pith of his soul lived on in the recollections of discussions shared, the lives he had contacted, and the significant impact he had on the manner in which we associate with each other. In his passing, he remained a guiding light—an exemplification of perseverance through the force of true human connections.

Chapter 10

Persevering Through Echo

As the world pushed ahead, the takeoff of Sir Michael Parkinson was not the finish of his story but rather the start of another part—a getting through reverberation that resounded through existence. His heritage, painstakingly woven through many years of significant discussions, stayed as a guiding light for a long time into the future.

The effect of his earth-shattering meetings, delicate moxy, and ageless insight kept on resounding through the records of diversion history. His voice might have stopped; however, the reverberations of his chuckling, the rhythm of his inquiries, and the truthfulness of his communications waited in the hearts and brains of the people who had been moved by his presence.

The always-advancing scene of media and correspondence tracked down comfort in his heritage. As the computerized age introduced new stages and conceivable outcomes, his model remained a resolute guide—a relentless update that, underneath the innovative headways, continued the core of correspondence as before. The embodiment of human association, the force of compassion, and the sorcery of veritable discourse were ageless insights that rose above the moving tides of progress.

In the domains of meetings, television shows, digital broadcasts, and then some, Sir Michael's heritage kept on rousing another age of communicators. His methodology served as a guide for the people who tried to connect with, comprehend, and move through the craft of discussion. The universe of media embraced his lessons, making spaces where people could share their accounts, trade thoughts, and associate in manners that reverberated profoundly.

The world he had left behind was not a static one, but a no-nonsense embroidery that consumed his insight and kept on developing. With each interview directed in his soul, every snapshot of certifiable trade, his heritage turned into a necessary string woven into the texture of human experience.

As time pushed ahead, the persevering reverberation of Sir Michael Parkinson's heritage remained. It was an update that even in a universe of speedy change, a few bits of insight stayed steady: the significance of tuning in, the force of legitimacy, and the magnificence of shared stories. His life was a demonstration of the possibility that each discussion, each trade, could have an effect—a wave that stretched out a long way past the occasion.

Thus, his story proceeded—a continuous exchange that extended across time and ages. His heritage was not a static artifact but rather a living demonstration of the specialty of discussion, a greeting for all to draw in, associate with, and motivate—to make their own reverberations in the huge span of the human experience.

Epilogue

A Goodbye and Reflection

In the immense embroidery of time, the tale of Sir Michael Parkinson remained a brilliant guide—a wellspring of motivation that rose above periods and ages. His excursion, which started as an inquisitive Yorkshire kid and finished in the knighthood of a media legend, had made a permanent imprint on the universe of correspondence, everlastingly modifying the manner in which humankind drew in with one another.

As admirers and supporters pondered the sections of his life, they found comfort in the recollections he had woven—each meeting, each sincere trade, remaining as a demonstration of the significant effect of credible human association. With a voice that reverberated past screens and stages, he had demonstrated that discussions held the ability to connect holes, to join hearts, and to enlighten the common encounters that bound humankind together.

From the unobtrusive starting points of his Yorkshire childhood to the great phases of worldwide acknowledgment, Sir Michael's process typified the substance of flexibility, interest, and sympathy. He had deftly explored the perplexing dance of life—handling difficulties sincerely, encouraging associations through discourse, and leaving a permanent engraving on the texture of mankind's set of experiences.

The discussions he had unbelievably led were not simply temporary minutes; they were ageless stories that rose above the requirements of existence. With each inquiry he posed and each story he shared, he had added to an orchestra of human encounters—an ensemble that resounded as the years progressed, interfacing spirits across continents and ages.

As admirers thought back on his life, they wound up attracted to the legitimacy that had been portrayed in his communications. His inheritance wasn't just about the words verbally expressed; it was about the associations shaped, the comprehension acquired, and the certifiable compassion he displayed. As the years progressed, he gifted the world with a mother lode of experiences, giggling, and genuine minutes that would keep on contacting lives long into what was in store.

Thus, as the sun set on his actual presence, the memory of Sir Michael Parkinson remained a persistent sign of the effect one individual could have. His process had been in excess of a progression of achievements; it had been a demonstration of the specialty of discussion, the wizardry of association, and the magnificence of being genuinely present at the time.

As time proceeded with its constant walk forward, the examples of Sir Michael's life remained—a greeting for all to draw in with each other legitimately, to tune in with an open heart, and to perceive the significant excellence in the tales that make up the human experience. His heritage was a murmured guarantee that discussions held the ability to shape fates, encourage understanding, and enlighten the limitless embroidery of humankind.